How many days of the week can be extraordinary?

Acknowledgements
The quotations in this book were gathered lovingly but unscientifically over several years and/or were contributed by many friends or acquaintances. Some arrived—and survived in our files—on scraps of paper and may therefore be imperfectly worded or attributed. To the authors, contributors, and original sources, our thanks, and where appropriate, our apologies. ~The Editors

With special thanks to the entire Compendium family.

Credits:
Written & Compiled by: Dan Zadra & Kobi Yamada
Designed by: Steve Potter
Edited by: Jennifer Pletsch & M.H. Clark
Creative Direction by: Sarah Forster

ISBN 978-1-93541417-9

3rd printing. Printed in China with soy inks.

Life moves pretty quickly these days.

We make time for work and other obligations, and that's important. But we forget sometimes that life is not just an obligation, it's an adventure.

Each day of the week comes to us with gifts and possibilities in its hands, but because of our routines we often don't see them or can't reach out to them. In our rush to make a living, we forget to live.

Happiness is in Your Hands

Choose life! Only that and always! At whatever risk. To let life leak out, to let it wear away by the mere passage of time, to withhold giving and spending it is to choose nothing.
~Sister Helen Kelly

Down deep inside, we all know that life is not a race to be run; it's a journey to be savored every step of the way. Whatever happened to simple pleasures and spontaneous experiences? Where are the little interludes in your day for loving, laughing, loafing, or learning? When did you lose the right to do something wonderful for yourself, your loved ones, or your community— not just now and then, but every day if you wish?

This is not a work book, it's a play book. It's not a book of instructions or answers, it's a book of inspirations, questions, and reminders. Simply put, the 7 book is a fun tool to reconnect with all the good things that are truly important to you. To help you rediscover the joy, passion, purpose, and meaning in every day of your week.

Look around. Life is here, and it is now. We can't let it simply slip away. Possibilities for adventure, beauty, contribution, and goodness are every-where—and you really can make time for them. Let the ideas in these pages guide and inspire you. Remember, happiness is always in your hands.

30,000 mornings

30,000 mornings, give or take, is all we're given. If you're 26, you still have 20,000 left. If you're 54, you still have 10,000. An accident or illness could change all that, of course. But let's count on you to remain safe and healthy all your allotted life—in which case you still have plenty of time. Sort of. "We get to think of life as an inexhaustible well," wrote author Paul Bowles, who lived to the ripe old age of 32,442 mornings. "Yet everything happens only a certain number of times, and a very small number, really. How many more times will you remember a certain afternoon of your childhood, some afternoon that's so deeply a part of your being that you can't even conceive of your life without it? Perhaps four or five times more, perhaps not even that. How many more times will you watch the full moon rise? Perhaps twenty. And yet it all seems limitless." 30,000 mornings. We'll spend some of them on the treadmill, or fighting traffic, or standing in line at the bagel shop. Just be sure to spend some of yours seeking and savoring the real beauty, mystery, and adventure of your days. This is your life; don't miss a day of it.

...there are three things we all should do every day. We should do this every day of our lives. Number one is laugh. You should laugh every day. Number two is think. You should spend some time in thought. Number three is, you should have your emotions moved to tears, could be happiness or joy. But think about it. If you laugh, you think, and you cry, that's a full day. That's a heck of a day. You do that seven days a week, you're going to have something special.

~Jim Valvano, college basketball coach, from his ESPY Awards speech, given just eight weeks before he died of cancer

time flies

In the early 1980s, I attended a conference in Southern California where I happened to hear a woman, a Canadian environmentalist, speak on her 95th birthday. I have long since forgotten her name, but her message has stuck with me all my life.

This woman, whom I'll call Catherine, shared this wise and wonderful advice with a group of aspiring young Forest Service workers:

"They say life is short, but is it? Once you get close to 100, people will ask you point-blank if life seems short or long when you look back on it. Today, I have decided to let the cat out of the bag.

"Somewhere in my thirties, the pace of life began to quicken," Catherine continued. "I was so busy trying to raise a family and fund my reforestation projects that whole years began to fly by in a blur, as if I wasn't even there for them. It seemed like only a short time passed before I looked up and saw my 70th birthday coming at me like a runaway train. In that regard, I can tell you that life from birth to 70 was far too short, at least for me."

In contrast, Catherine said that her life from 70 to 95 had seemed longer, fuller, richer and more beautiful—almost spiritual. What had changed? Just one thing: "I made a conscious decision to live those years one day a time," she explained. "It dawned on me that life is short, but the days are long if you are conscious of them. The secret is this, and please don't wait until it's too late to learn it:

"Live consciously. Treat each day as if it's a miniature lifetime. In this way I have learned to get more life out of one day than I used to get out of entire years."

Time is a very precious gift...so precious that it is only given to us moment by moment.
~Amelia Barr

KNOW NOTHING. APPRECIATE EVERYTHING.

Become a beginner again.

We lose something wonderful when it becomes more important to us to be the one who knows than to be the one who's open to the everyday wonders around us. "Those who think they know it all have no way of finding out they don't," wrote Leo Buscaglia. Fortunately, our sense of curiosity and wonder can be rekindled and refreshed.

Artists and photographers are taught to observe the world through the eyes of a child. "Every child is an artist," said Pablo Picasso. "The problem is how to remain an artist once we grow up."

Inventors and product developers are taught to see things as an amateur would, rather than as an expert. An expert looks at two spoons and sees two spoons; an amateur looks at two spoons and sees a musical instrument.

Zen practitioners are taught to approach every moment of life with a "beginner's mind." As Abbess Zenkei Blanche Hartman says, this is a "mind innocent of preconceptions and expectations, judgments and prejudices." It's a mind full of curiosity, wonder, and amazement. The beginner's mind revels in being naïve and not knowing.

Imagine seeing everything as if for the first time.

It was Saint Patrick's Day. Another cold, gray, blustery Tuesday morning in Seattle. I was behind on a project and should've been at work, and my seven-year-old daughter, Rosie, should've been in school. Instead, the two of us were all bundled up and on our way to a grassy meadow behind a neighbor's house—an enchanted-looking cluster of knolls where (according to my neighbor, at least) real leprechauns had recently been sighted.

Quietly, so as not to frighten the leprechauns, Rosie and I crept to the top of a knoll that day and settled down, side by side, with our backs against a big maple tree. For two or three hours, it was just Rosie and me. Sipping hot chocolate from a thermos to ward off the cold, we held our vigil, keeping our eyes peeled for the slightest movement in the long grass down by the willows.

"Rosie, did you see that?!" I whispered. "Look over there where the path ends—can you see anything?" Her eyes grew wide. By now, we were both catching glimpses of little green hats and boots flitting all around us. "Now, do you believe?" I asked her in a hushed tone, because, as everyone knows, leprechauns only appear to those who believe. Of course, by then she certainly did believe, and I guess I did too.

Then came the most magical moment of all. Late in the morning we wandered along the edge of the meadow, pushing gently at the grass with our shoe tips, hoping for one last sign of a leprechaun burrow. And then—wonder of wonders—Rosie suddenly stumbled upon a cache of real Irish pennies and some chocolate coins covered in gold foil! Someone (a genuine leprechaun, perhaps?) had apparently dropped those coins in the grass the night before.

It was just another rainy Tuesday in Seattle for most people, but not for me and Rosie. And, despite playing hooky that morning back in 1992, Rosie made it through grade school okay, and today she has a great job. As for me, I've long since forgotten whatever project I was supposed to be working on. But Rosie and I will never forget that magical day in March when we lay in wait for the leprechauns together.

Many years later, on Saint Patrick's Day, Rosie paid a visit to Seattle and surprised me with a card and a present. It was a cupful of gold-covered chocolate coins with a hand-written note tucked inside: "Dad, Happy Saint Patrick's Day. I still believe."

That little note remains one of my most treasured possessions.

Do you still believe?

The work will wait until you show the child the rainbow, but the rainbow won't wait until the work is done.
~Patricia Clifford

Most of the time, we barely look at an apple we are eating. We grab it, take a bite, chew quickly, and swallow. In his inspiring book, *Savor*, Thich Nhat Hanh describes a simple "apple meditation" to remind us how to approach and appreciate every experience in a more mindful state. The next time you eat an apple…

Hold onto it for a moment. What kind of apple is it? What color is it? How does it feel in your hand? What does it smell like?

Give the apple a smile and slowly take a bite. What does it feel like in your mouth? What does it taste like? What is it like to chew and swallow it?

Truly savor all the qualities the apple is offering you: its sweetness, aroma, freshness, juiciness, crispness.

There is nothing else filling your mind as you chew—no projects, no deadlines, no worries, no to-do lists, no fears, no sorrows, no anger, no past, no future. Just this apple.

In this way you appreciate the apple as it is. You become fully aware of eating the apple, and you become fully engaged in the here and now. By living in the moment you become more alive. If you can savor the apple, you can savor your life.

Inhabit your moments.

The little things in life aren't little.

SUNNY SATURDAYS. A CALL FROM AN OLD FRIEND. HOMEMADE TREATS. GROWING SOMETHING FROM SEED. COOPERATION. CLEAN SHEETS. MEALS WITH FAMILY. SOLVING A PROBLEM. AN UNEXPECTED PACKAGE IN THE MAIL. FEELING APPRECIATED. BERRY PICKING. BLOWING BUBBLES. TEAMWORK. SUDDEN INSPIRATION. A SIMPLE ACT OF KINDNESS. A BRISK WALK. GOOD NEWS. CHILDREN'S LAUGHTER. LEMONADE STANDS. LONG WEEKENDS. PERFECT TIMING. HAPPY ACCIDENTS. NEW POSSIBILITIES. MUSIC PLAYING THROUGH AN OPEN WINDOW. MAKING SOMETHING FROM SCRATCH. BLUE SKIES. NICE NEIGHBORS. GRATITUDE. HOT COFFEE ON A CAMPING TRIP. THE FIRST TRUE DAY OF SPRING. A PERFECT PEACH. KITE FLYING. FRESH BREAD. GOING BAREFOOT. SEEING A SHOOTING STAR. A WELL-EARNED COMPLIMENT. SURPRISE PARTIES. MAKING PROGRESS. GENEROSITY. FRESH AIR. BEING A PART OF SOMETHING GOOD. THE SMELL OF AN EVERGREEN. DEEP BREATHS. TOTAL RELAXATION. BEAR HUGS. PICNICS. THE SOUND OF THE OCEAN. REAL MAPLE SYRUP. BRILLIANT AUTUMN LEAVES. PUPPIES. GRACE. GETTING INVOLVED. GIVING BACK. HOLDING HANDS. TREE SWINGS. FREE AFTERNOONS. CANDLELIT DINNERS. MAKING SOMEONE'S DAY. CATNAPS. PHOTO BOOTHS. FINDING SOMETHING TO BE PASSIONATE ABOUT. THE SMELL OF FRESHLY CUT GRASS. SMALL VICTORIES. THE RIGHT WORDS AT THE RIGHT TIME. HELPING SOMEONE IN NEED. ROAD TRIPS. PORCH SWINGS. A NEW FRIEND. A GREAT GOAL TO WORK FOR. A REUNION AT THE AIRPORT. DRAWINGS DONE IN SIDEWALK CHALK. MOMENTS OF PEACE. CONTAGIOUS ENTHUSIASM. POSITIVE CHANGE. RAINBOWS. A LONG, HOT BATH. DOING SOMETHING TO BE PROUD OF. RELIVING A WONDERFUL MEMORY. A FAVORITE SONG ON THE RADIO. TAKING THE SCENIC ROUTE. FAVORITE TRADITIONS. MORNING BIRDSONG. FOUR-LEAF CLOVERS. THINGS THAT ARE MEANT TO BE SHARED. TANDEM BICYCLES. BEING THERE FOR SOMEONE ELSE. SUMMER RAINSTORMS. GLITTER. LADYBUGS. A GOOD NIGHT'S SLEEP. A NEW CHALLENGE. FEELING HEALTHY. KNOWING YOU'VE DONE YOUR BEST. SHARING A LAUGH. A SENSE OF ACCOMPLISHMENT. SAND BETWEEN YOUR TOES. WORDS OF ENCOURAGEMENT. SPLASHING IN PUDDLES. A SUDDEN FIT OF THE GIGGLES. OPEN MINDS. FINDING FORGOTTEN POCKET CHANGE. LISTENING TO THE RAIN ON THE ROOF. BIG-HEARTED PEOPLE. MAKING A DIFFERENCE.

Passion & Purpose

Finding your real purpose or passion is like searching all over the house for your car keys, only to discover that they were in your own hands all the time.

If you ask most people what their purpose is in life, they either don't know or feel as if they have to give an impressive answer like finding the cure for cancer, writing the great American novel, or ending world hunger.

A great way to pinpoint your purpose is to simply pay attention to yourself rather than to what you think other people want to hear. "Seek out that particular attribute which makes you feel most deeply and vitally alive," wrote William James, "along with which comes the inner voice which says, 'This is the real me,' and when you have found that…follow it."

There's a TV commercial that shows a man building birdhouses in his shop. The little houses are like works of art—all very colorful and intricate and beautiful. The music dies down, he looks at the camera and says, "I plan on making birdhouses the rest of my life."

His honest passion for his calling makes you wish that you loved something that way, too. Well, down deep in your heart, you *do* love something that way. That something is the real you, and it *will* call out to you. Listen closely.

"Listen to the clues," wrote Steve Chandler. "The next time you feel real joy, stop and think. Pay attention. Because joy is the universe's way of knocking on your mind's door. Hello in there. Is anyone home? Can I leave a message? Yes? Good! The message is that you are happy, and that means that you are in touch with your purpose."

Put your ear down close to your soul and listen hard. ~Anne Sexton

For the past 30 years, I have looked in the mirror every morning and asked myself: "If today were the last day of my life, would I want to do what I am about to do today?" And whenever the answer has been "no" for too many days in a row, I know I need to change something.

~Steve Jobs, Apple Chairman, from a commencement speech at Stanford University

Set your course by the stars, not by the lights of every passing ship. ~Omar Bradley

FOLLOW YOUR

One of the wisest principles of lifetime happiness and peace of mind is so obvious that we sometimes forget it—and, in the forgetting, we lose our way. The principle is this: **Live each day in alignment with your values.**

Your values are the choices you make about what's most important to you. Living your life by your values is like establishing true north on a compass. From then on, the compass knows only one point—its ideal—and it will guide you through the darkest nights and fiercest storms.

You may know what your values are. You may believe your values are your guiding stars. But if you aren't actually living your values—following your true north—chances are you won't ever be really happy, and your journey through life will feel spiritually off track.

The good news is that you don't have to wait a single minute to start realigning your life with your values—and the rewards will convince you to make it a lifelong commitment.

TRUE NORTH

Am I living my life in integrity with my values?
If you say you value your health, are you still smoking or out of shape?
If you say you value your family, are you spending more time with them?
If you say you value adventure, are you taking your vacations?

My top values are:

_____

_____

_____

_____

_____

_____

I am currently. . .

☐ living this value

☐ living this value

☐ living this value

☐ living this value

☐ living this value

☐ living this value

☐ living this value

Ways I will commit to my values this week that will put me on course to my true north:

_____

_____

_____

_____

_____

_____

If you want a great life, ask great questions. Questions can be catalysts. They serve as challenges, inspirations, road maps, hints of something better, calls to action, and new beginnings. If you want better answers for your life, try asking better questions. Instead of asking, why me, why am I so unhappy, or what's wrong with me, try asking, how can I make this work, how can I make a difference, or what am I grateful for?

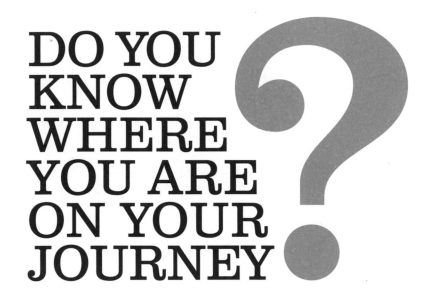

LIVING
BACKWARDS

The purpose of life can't possibly be chronic busyness, obsessive money making or status chasing.

True, many people initially go to work to make money or make a name, but they always discover in the end that this didn't really make them happy. Turn it around! Try being and doing whatever makes you really happy and fulfilled—pursue your purpose—and you will inevitably find that money and success will follow.

Author Margaret Young put it this way: "Often people attempt to live their lives backwards, they try to have more things, or more money in order to do more of what they want so they will be happier. The way it actually works is the reverse. You must first be who you really are, then do what you need to do, in order to have what you want."

Am I living my life by "have...do...be?" or "be...do...have?"

Every day, at the stroke of midnight, exactly 86,400 seconds of life are deposited into your own personal time account. They are your most valuable possession. How many moments will move you? How many will be memorable? You are the one who ultimately decides how you will spend your time. Each moment is here for you to use and enjoy. And any portion of your time that you neglect to use during any 24-hour period is lost and gone forever.

Too busy for life?

A *USA Today* poll asked Americans, "How busy are you?" The majority replied, "I am busier today than I was last year, and I was busier last year than I was the year before. And I sacrifice friends, family and sleep for my success."

When Americans were asked, "What would you do if you had an 8-day week instead of a 7-day week?" most, unfortunately, did not answer with things like: "I would play with my kids. I'd get to know my neighbors. I would enjoy a hobby that's rewarding and relaxing. I would spend more time with friends." Instead, most answered that they would use that extra day to catch up at work.

Source: Professor Philip Zimbardo

What would you do
with an extra day?

3 2 4 6

WARNING:

Dates in calendar are closer than they appear.

~Unknown

LESS IS MORE.

WHILE AT WALDEN POND, HENRY DAVID THOREAU DECIDED NOT TO GET A RUG FOR HIS LITTLE CABIN. IF HE GOT A RUG, HE WOULD HAVE TO GET A RUG BEATER; AND IF HE GOT A RUG BEATER, HE WOULD HAVE TO GET A RUG HOOK TO HANG IT ON. HE COULD SEE WHERE THAT MIGHT LEAD...

THOREAU BELIEVED THAT ACQUIRING MORE THINGS DID NOT NECESSARILY EQUATE TO MORE JOY. TODAY, SOPHISTICATED STUDIES CONFIRM WHAT THOREAU AND MANY OTHER WISE SOULS FIGURED OUT ON THEIR OWN: INSTEAD OF PUTTING THINGS FIRST, PEOPLE ENJOY A RICHER LIFE WHEN THEY PUT EXPERIENCES FIRST.

HOW ABOUT YOU? IF YOU ONLY HAVE SO MUCH LIFE TO INVEST, HOW DO YOU REALLY WANT TO SPEND IT? DO YOU WANT TO SPEND IT DRIVING TO THE MALL TO BUY MORE STUFF? OR WOULD YOU RATHER INVEST IT IN EXPERIENCING THE GREAT BARRIER REEF WITH YOUR BEST FRIEND? OR BIKING THE HIAWATHA TRAIL WITH YOUR KIDS? OR MAYBE GETTING OUT AND GIVING BACK TO YOUR COMMUNITY?

MORE AND MORE PEOPLE ARE DISCOVERING THE ART OF TRAVELING LIGHT IN LIFE.

LIVE SIMPLY, LOVE LAVISHLY.

Things I can eliminate this week:
(So I can make more time and room for what really matters.)

1 —————————————————————————

2 —————————————————————————

3 —————————————————————————

4 —————————————————————————

5 —————————————————————————

6 —————————————————————————

7 —————————————————————————

How many are the things I can do without!
~Socrates

How we spend our days is, of course,

how we
spend
our lives.

~Annie Dillard

One day a philosophy professor brought a large glass jar and some beautiful river rocks to class with him. "Raise your hands when the jar is full," he instructed his students, and he began putting the big rocks into the jar. Soon the lid would no longer fit, and all the students raised their hands to indicate the jar was full. The professor then pulled out a bag of smaller black and white pebbles and poured them into the jar. As the pebbles rolled down, they filled in the little gaps between the big river rocks. The students smiled and raised their hands. This time the jar was completely full. Then the professor produced a bag of sand and began pouring it into the jar. When the sand had filled the tiny gaps between the rocks and the pebbles he triumphantly placed the lid on the jar and asked his class if the jar was now full. They all clapped and agreed, "Yes, it is full!" At that point, the professor opened the lid and slowly poured two cups of coffee into the jar. The coffee completely filled the tiniest gaps between the rocks, the pebbles, and the grains of sand. "Now, life is very much like this jar," he said. The river rocks represent the most important things in life, such as your ethics, your family, your loved ones, your health. Even if you lost everything else, your life would still be full with these most important things in it. The pebbles are the things in our lives that are pretty important—but our happiness shouldn't depend on them. Things like our job, house, car, etc. Finally, the sand represents everything else—the countless small, busy things in our lives. If we fill up our jar with sand first, then we won't have any room for the river rocks or pebbles. If we fill our lives with just the small stuff or the busy stuff, we won't have any room or time for the things that mean the most to us." After a brief moment of silence one of the students asked, "Professor, what does the coffee represent?" "Ah, I'm glad you asked," replied the professor. "It means that no matter how full your life is, there is always room for a cup of coffee with a friend."

What am I putting first?

What currently occupies the most space in my life?

Which things should be my true river rocks?

Which pebbles or sand am I devoting too much time to?

Who should I take to coffee this week?

We will always have time for the things we put first. ~Liane Steele

Listen, are you breathing just a little

and calling it a life?

~Mary Oliver

THERE ARE NO
HAVE TO'S IN LIFE…

I can't go skydiving,
I have to be practical.

I can't go to my
niece's graduation,
I have to work.

I can't attend my high
school reunion,
I have to lose weight.

I can't hike Machu Picchu
this summer,
I have to paint the house.

When it comes right down to it, there are very few have to's in life. You have to be born, and you have to die. In between, the rest of your life is pretty much up to you.

Why build a prison for yourself with have to's, can'ts, or they won't let me's? Instead, guide your life with I can, I want to, I choose to, I can't wait to…

I can ....

I want to ....

I choose to ....

I can't wait to ....

We become happier, much happier, when we realize
that life is an opportunity rather than an obligation.

~Mary Augustine

DON'T SPEND YOUR PRECIOUS TIME ASKING, **"WHY ISN'T THE WORLD A BETTER PLACE?"** IT WILL ONLY BE TIME WASTED. THE QUESTION TO ASK IS **"HOW CAN I MAKE IT BETTER?"** TO THAT THERE IS AN ANSWER.

~LEO BUSCAGLIA

NO MATTER WHAT YOU HOPE TO DO IN THE

FUTURE, THERE'S NOTHING STOPPING YOU

FROM TRANSFORMING YOUR CURRENT JOB

INTO A MORE MEANINGFUL AND PURPOSEFUL

EXPERIENCE RIGHT NOW. ROBERT HOLDEN,

Changing your business card to a mission card

THE AUTHOR OF *BE HAPPY*, ENCOURAGES

PEOPLE TO SIT DOWN AND DRAW UP THEIR

OWN UNIQUE BUSINESS CARDS. INSTEAD OF

WRITING YOUR JOB TITLE ON THIS CARD, WRITE

DOWN THE HIGHER PURPOSE OR MISSION OF

YOUR WORK. THE IDEA IS TO IDENTIFY THE

PART OF YOUR CURRENT WORK THAT MAKES

YOU FEEL FULFILLED RATHER THAN JUST BUSY.

A hair stylist's job
could become:

SELF-ESTEEM CONSULTANT

The purpose of my work is to help people feel good about themselves.

A taxi driver's job
could become:

ROVING AMBASSADOR

The purpose of my work is to provide a warm welcome and leave a great impression on people traveling our city.

My current job
could become:

MY NEW JOB TITLE:

_____

The purpose or mission of my work:

If it's not fun, why do it?

Ben & Jerry's is a quirky but wildly successful ice cream company, renowned for its offbeat marketing and for donating a portion of its profits to good causes. Two lifelong friends, Ben Cohen and Jerry Greenfield, started the company in a converted gas station in Vermont with nothing but $12,000 and a great sense of humor. Over the years, Ben and Jerry created the world's largest ice cream sundae (more than 13 tons!), launched their famous Cowmobile (a converted motor home that handed out free scoops of Ben & Jerry's across the country), delivered a 900-pound baked Alaska to the U.S. Capitol Building, and raised millions of dollars for community action causes through their foundation. Since most of us spend a third of our lives at work, Ben and Jerry reasoned that work should be both fun and a positive force for good.

Year after year, Southwest Airlines achieves some of the lowest employee turnover and the highest customer satisfaction rates in the airline industry. Here are some of the maxims that guide the company's approach to business:

HIRE PEOPLE WITH A SENSE OF HUMOR

ENCOURAGE PEOPLE TO ADOPT A PLAYFUL ATTITUDE

BE THE FIRST TO LAUGH

LAUGH WITH, NOT AT

TAKE WORK SERIOUSLY, BUT NOT YOURSELF

Good advice for all of us.

Take work seriously, but not yourself.

At age 87, Mick Carlson advised his son, "All my life there's been one little rule that has worked wonderfully for me: If there's any area of your life in which you are less than 50 percent happy, make an immediate change."

What percentage of happiness would you currently assign to the significant areas of your life?

BEETHOVEN used to leave his studio and wander the streets or the woods to find his music. Out in the fresh air he could hear new symphonies in the studio of his mind.

EINSTEIN visualized his Theory of Relativity ($E = MC^2$), not at his desk at the patent office, but while taking a ride through the city on a subway.

Take lots of field trips

The imagination needs moodling—long, inefficient happy idling, dawdling, and puttering. ~Brenda Ueland

MARY ANDERSON, while sightseeing in New York City, noticed that drivers had to open the windows of their cars when it rained in order to see—so she invented the windshield wiper.

ANN MOORE, while traveling with the Peace Corps, noticed African mothers carrying their babies in hands-free fabric slings. Inspired, she returned to the United States and invented the original Snugli baby carrier.

NOLAN BUSHNELL came up with the idea for his iconic *Breakout* computer game while running his fingers through sand at the beach.

SOMEDAY

IS NOT A DAY OF THE WEEK

One of our greatest illusions is that someday we will have more time to take action on our dreams and aspirations. But one thing leads to another, and someday never comes. While we are busy postponing things, life speeds by.

There's something (or several somethings) you've been wanting to do, try, or launch but just haven't gotten around to. Why are you waiting? A dream without action is just a wish.

At last I think I've discovered the secret: Do whatever your heart leads you to do—but do it!

~Truman X. Jones

Have you been dreaming of touching the Great Wall of China? Writing your first book? Starting your own business? Great.

Today is the day to get started on making your dream a reality. It's easier to do one small action now instead of some grand action *someday*.

Today I will...

"The tragedy of life," said W.M. Lewis, "is not that it ends so soon, but that we wait so long to begin it."

MISTAKES ARE GREA+

Without risk, nothing new ever happens. Live life fully while you're here. Experience everything. Try new things. Enjoy yourself, be crazy, be daring. Don't hold back! Get out of your comfort zone. And, every now and then, bite off more than you can chew.

You'll make mistakes. So what? If you aren't making mistakes, you aren't really living. Besides, studies indicate that people who don't take risks generally make about two big mistakes a year…and people who do take risks make about the same number—so why hold back on life or fear the attempt?

IF YOU AREN'T MAKING SOME MISTAKES, YOU AREN'T TAKING ENOUGH CHANCES. ~JOHN SCULLEY MISTAKES ARE A PART OF THE DUES ONE PAYS FOR A FULL LIFE. ~SOPHIA LOREN IF I HAD MY LIFE TO LIVE OVER, I'D DARE TO MAKE MORE MISTAKES NEXT TIME. ~NADINE STAIR A MISTAKE IS SIMPLY ANOTHER WAY OF DOING THINGS. ~KATHARINE GRAHAM CREATIVITY IS ALLOWING YOURSELF TO MAKE MISTAKES. ART IS KNOWING WHICH ONES TO KEEP. ~SCOTT ADAMS ADMITTING A MISTAKE JUST MEANS THAT YOU ARE WISER TODAY THAN YOU WERE YESTERDAY. ~KELLY ROTHAUS AN EXPERT IS SIMPLY A PERSON WHO HAS MADE ALL THE MISTAKES THAT CAN BE MADE IN A RELATIVELY NARROW FIELD. ~NIELS BOHR THERE ARE NO MISTAKES, THERE ARE ONLY LEARNINGS AND YEARNINGS. ~JUNE MARTIN DON'T BE AFRAID TO DO IT WRONG, BE AFRAID NOT TO HAVE MADE THE ATTEMPT. ~JAMES PATTERSON THE ONLY PERSON WHO NEVER MAKES MISTAKES IS THE PERSON WHO NEVER DOES ANYTHING. ~DENIS WAITLEY NO MORE MISTAKES AND YOU'RE THROUGH. ~JOHN CLEESE TO OBTAIN MAXIMUM ATTENTION, IT'S HARD TO BEAT A GOOD, BIG MISTAKE. ~YOGI BERRA WHENEVER YOU UNDERTAKE SOMETHING NEW, ATTEMPT TO MAKE MANY MISTAKES AS RAPIDLY AS POSSIBLE IN ORDER TO LEARN AS MUCH AS YOU CAN IN A SHORT PERIOD OF TIME. ~BOB MOAWAD FROM ERROR TO ERROR ONE DISCOVERS THE ENTIRE TRUTH. ~SIGMUND FREUD A MISTAKE ONLY PROVES THAT SOMEONE STOPPED TALKING LONG ENOUGH TO ACTUALLY DO SOMETHING. ~MICHAEL LEBOEUF DO NOT FEAR MISTAKES, THERE ARE NONE. ~MILES DAVIS IF YOU HAVE MADE MISTAKES, THERE IS ALWAYS ANOTHER CHANCE FOR YOU. YOU MAY HAVE A FRESH START ANY MOMENT YOU CHOOSE, FOR THIS THING WE CALL "FAILURE" IS NOT THE FALLING DOWN, BUT THE STAYING DOWN. ~MARY PICKFORD EVEN THE KNOWLEDGE OF MY OWN FALLIBILITY CANNOT KEEP ME FROM MAKING MISTAKES. ONLY WHEN I FALL DO I GET UP AGAIN. ~VINCENT VAN GOGH FREEDOM IS NOT WORTH HAVING IF IT DOES NOT CONNOTE FREEDOM TO ERR. ~MAHATMA GANDHI AN INTELLIGENT PERSON IS NEVER AFRAID OR ASHAMED TO FIND ERRORS IN HIS UNDERSTANDING OF THINGS. ~BRYANT H. MCGILL YOU MUST LEARN FROM THE MISTAKES OF OTHERS. YOU CAN'T POSSIBLY LIVE LONG ENOUGH TO MAKE THEM ALL YOURSELF. ~SAM LEVENSON I AM GLAD THAT I PAID SO LITTLE ATTENTION TO GOOD ADVICE; HAD I ABIDED BY IT I MIGHT HAVE BEEN SAVED FROM SOME OF MY MOST VALUABLE MISTAKES. ~EDNA ST. VINCENT MILLAY DO NOT BE EMBARRASSED BY YOUR MISTAKES. NOTHING CAN TEACH US BETTER THAN OUR UNDERSTANDING OF THEM. THIS IS ONE OF THE BEST WAYS OF SELF-EDUCATION. ~THOMAS CARLYLE MISTAKES ARE A FACT OF LIFE. IT IS THE RESPONSE TO ERROR THAT COUNTS. ~NIKKI GIOVANNI

CHANGE YOUR MIND. CHANGE YOUR LIFE.

We all have these worn-out beliefs, preconceptions, or prejudices that we unconsciously haul around with us. Usually they have nothing to do with reality, and yet we carry them still, even as they negatively impact our lives. For centuries, seafaring people believed that the world was flat and that you would fall off the edge if you sailed too far. That belief had nothing to do with reality, but it still placed an artificial limit on adventure, discovery, and a better life for millions of people.

All personal discoveries or breakthroughs begin with a change of mind or heart. "Every day," wrote Brazilian novelist Paulo Coelho, "God gives us the sun and also a moment in which we have the ability to change everything that makes us unhappy. Our magic moment helps us change and sends us off in search of our dreams."

You think you can't do math or learn a musical instrument? Change your mind. You think you can't get along with your sister, your neighbor, or your father-in-law? Change your mind. You think you can't travel the world, follow a dream, or change your life for the better? Change your mind and you change your life.

Don't ask yourself what the world needs. Ask yourself what makes you come alive, and go do that, because what the world needs is people who have come alive.

~Howard Thurman

Since the dawn of history, people have been searching for the meaning of life.

Some say that life is a problem to be solved; others say it's a mystery to be experienced.

Some say it's a test to be endured; others say it's a gift to be enjoyed.

Some say it's an opportunity to build an empire; others say it's a chance to grow a soul.

In his lifelong study of myth and bliss in different cultures, Joseph Campbell looked at men and women across history and around the world, and concluded:

"I don't believe people are looking for the meaning of life as much as they are looking for the experience of being alive."

Novelist Joyce Carol Oates put it even simpler: "We are here to feel the joy of life pulsing in us now." Not someday, right now. At this very moment, there are people who have essentially stopped living. They aren't outwardly complaining, or searching for inspiration, or voicing their frustration; they're merely waiting for time to pass.

Gretchen Rubin, writer of *The Happiness Project,* urges each of us to stop now and then and hold a meeting with ourselves to explore this important question:
"From 0 to 10, how alive do I feel?"

Zero represents the living dead, and 10 represents fully alive.

| 0 | 1 | 2 | 3 | 4 | 5 | 6 | 7 | 8 | 9 | 10 |

When was the last time I felt really alive, and what was I doing?

_____

_____

_____

_____

What are seven activities, pleasures, or events that will make me feel even more alive—right now, this week?

1 _____

2 _____

3 _____

4 _____

5 _____

6 _____

7 _____

AT THE BEGINNING OF EVERY DAY,

ask yourself how you can make today

a day you'll wish you could relive again

years from now.

AT THE END OF EVERY DAY,
take a quiet moment to give
thanks. Say thank you for all
you've done, given, dreamed,
said, created, loved, survived,
learned, attempted, overcome,
savored, and enjoyed throughout your day.

a perfect

WHERE ARE YOU?

WHAT ARE YOU DOING?

WHO ARE YOU WITH?

HOW DO YOU FEEL?

WHAT DO YOU SEE?

WHERE WILL YOU GO NEXT?

HOW WILL YOU CREATE YOUR PERFECT DAY?

Brighten your little corner of the world.

Startled by a dream he had in which he saw himself as a softly glowing beam of light moving endlessly through a huge crowd, a man decided to adopt this vision as a personal philosophy. And his life was never the same.

"I can't control how people are treated in the world," he said, "but I can control how they are treated in my little corner of it.

"Each day, I know for certain that I can bring a little warmth and light to anyone who comes within my personal '10-foot zone.' My philosophy is that everyone has their own 10-foot zone. What a world this will be when all those little 10-foot beams of light finally branch and connect."

Light up your 10-foot zone

This week, be aware of all that takes place (or doesn't take place) in your personal 10-foot zone, Brighten your little corner of the world. It takes so little to shed light on someone we encounter in our day, but it can mean so much.

Be a lamp, or a lifeboat, or a ladder. Help someone's soul...

~Rumi

Everything Matters

> *There are generations yet unborn whose very lives will be shifted and shaped by the moves you make and the actions you take today.*
>
> *~Andy Andrews*

The Butterfly Effect: In the early 1960s, meteorologist Edward Lorenz presented a startling theory called the "butterfly effect" to the New York Academy of Science. Thirty years later, physics professors around the world verified the viability of this theory.

A butterfly flapping its wings can set air molecules in motion, which in turn can move more and more molecules of air, the gradual accumulation of which can create measureable changes in the atmosphere that could eventually alter, delay, accelerate or even prevent a tornado on the other side of the world.

In his book *The Butterfly Effect: How Your Life Matters*, author Andy Andrews shows how the principle of the butterfly effect applies to everything you do (or don't do).

Each day, from the time you warmly greet (or coldly ignore) your neighbor in the morning, to the time you patiently pet (or impetuously kick) your dog at night, every single thing you do throughout your day has an accumulating effect on something or someone else in the world—for good or bad. And it all matters.

Who are the "insignificant" people in your life?

This story appeared on the web one day and quickly made its way around the world. The author is unknown, but the reminder is beautiful and worth sharing.

During my second year of nursing school our professor gave us a pop quiz. I was a good student and breezed through the questions, until I read the last one: "What is the first name of the woman who cleans this school?"

Surely this was some kind of joke. I had seen the janitor in the hallways many times. She was tall, dark-haired, and probably in her fifties, but how would I know her name? I handed in my paper, leaving the last question blank. Before class ended, one student asked if the last question would actually count toward our quiz grade.

"Absolutely," said the professor. "During your career and your lifetime you will meet many people. Which ones are significant? All of them. They all deserve your attention and care, even if all you do is smile and say hello."

I've never forgotten that lesson. I also learned her name was Dorothy.

On December 14, 2005, the front page of the *San Francisco Chronicle* carried the story of a female humpback whale that had become entangled in a massive web of crab traps and lines. As she struggled to free herself, she soon had hundreds of yards of line wrapped around her body and tail.

A crab fisherman spotted her just east of the Farallon Islands (about 30 miles outside the Golden Gate) and radioed an environmental group for help. Within a matter of hours, the rescue team arrived and determined that the only way to save the whale was to physically dive in and untangle her. The divers worked for hours dangerously close to the whale and finally freed her.

Instead of making a hasty get away at this point, the whale made a surprising move. She swam in what seemed like joyous circles, coming up to each diver, one at a time, and gently nudging them, pushing some playfully around, as if she were thanking her rescuers.

Sometimes we think we do it all on our own. But for every accomplishment, there have been countless hands and hearts supporting us at every turn. The people who've loved, encouraged, helped, and believed in us—maybe even saved us—have been there all along.

There are people who have made your life brighter, your heart lighter. Have you told them how much you appreciate them?

give
thanks

7 people I want to thank this week:

_____

_____

_____

_____

_____

_____

_____

I see trees of green, red roses too,
I see them bloom, for me and you,
And I think to myself,
"What a wonderful world."
I see skies of blue, and clouds of white,
Bright blessed days, dark sacred nights,
And I think to myself,
"What a wonderful world."
The colors of the rainbow,
so pretty in the sky,
Are also on the faces
of people passing by,
I see friends shaking hands,
saying, "How do you do?"
They're really saying, "I love you."
I hear babies cry, and I watch them grow,
They'll learn much more
than I'll ever know.
And I think to myself,
"What a wonderful world."
Yes, I think to myself,
"What a wonderful world."

~George Weiss & Bob Thiele

That it will never come again
is what makes life so sweet.

~Emily Dickinson

They say, you only live once, but some people have figured out how to live their lives three times. Here's how it works:

First in anticipation, **second** in the actual moment, and, finally, **third** in recollection.

WHAT ARE YOU LOOKING FORWARD TO?

WHY NOT DESIGNATE SOME HOLIDAYS FOR YOURSELF EACH YEAR? THEY
CAN BE MOVABLE HOLIDAYS, SO YOU CAN ENJOY THEM WHENEVER YOU
REALLY NEED THEM THROUGHOUT THE YEAR. AND YOU CAN NAME THEM
WHATEVER YOU WANT. HOW ABOUT DAZZLE DAY OR DAWDLE DAY? OR
FILL-IN-THE-BLANK DAY?

THE IMPORTANT THING IS THAT YOU ARE FREE TO DO WHATEVER YOUR
HEART DESIRES ON YOUR SPECIAL DAY.

It's your

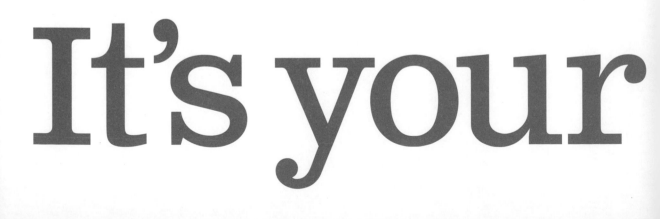

Ideas for your personal holiday

Wake up early.

See the sunrise.

Go back to bed.

Wake up again whenever.

Call in well.

Treat yourself to brunch at your favorite restaurant.

Wear flip-flops.

Visit a friend.

Go out and play.

Write a love letter.

Go to a matinee.

Catch an afternoon baseball game.

Call your mother.

Buy some flowers.

Visit the food bank.

Cook dinner for someone special.

Watch the sunset.

Count your blessings.

Life is an occasion. Rise to it.
~Mr. Magorium's Wonder Emporium

day!

Get out there.

JOHN MUIR, WHO FOUNDED THE SIERRA CLUB AND HELPED ESTABLISH YOSEMITE NATIONAL PARK, WANTED TO PRESERVE NATURE BECAUSE OF WHAT IT DID FOR THE HUMAN SPIRIT. HE SAID THAT MODERN LIFE "CHOKES THE SOUL," AND HE BELIEVED THAT WE COULD FIND OURSELVES BY GOING OUTSIDE AND CELEBRATING "GOD'S BIG SHOW."

NIKOS KAZANTZAKIS ONCE SAID THAT GOD CHANGES APPEARANCES EVERY SECOND AND WE SHOULD TRY TO RECOGNIZE HIM IN ALL HIS DISGUISES. ONE MOMENT HE IS A GLASS OF FRESH WATER; THE NEXT, YOUR SON BOUNCING ON YOUR KNEES OR THE SUNLIGHT ON AN EARLY MORNING WALK.

FIND A LITTLE PIECE OF HEAVEN ON EARTH, AND RETURN TO YOUR DAY A DIFFERENT PERSON—INSPIRED, REFRESHED, RESTORED.

Happiness…
not in another place, but this place, not for another hour, but this hour…

~WALT WHITMAN

WHAT KIND OF TIME IS IT?

In some Eastern, Polynesian, and Micronesian communities, the people don't tell you what time it is—they tell you what *kind* of time it is. Feast time. Fishing time. Helping time. Spirit time. Loving time. Lazy time. Children time. Old-people time. Moon time. Dream time. Each time of the day or week elicits a different way of seeing, feeling, walking, talking, and responding to an important facet of life. This week, try planning your days and nights according to your dreams and ideals, not just your watch.

Never lose a holy curiosity.

Stop every day to understand

and appreciate a little of the

mystery that surrounds you, and

your life will be filled with awe

and discovery to the very end.

~ALBERT EINSTEIN

Take time to marvel

The wonders of the world and
the universe are available to you right now.
They are everywhere and all around you—in the
intricate parts of your body, in the creative power of your
mind and imagination, in the vast expanses of space, and in
the marvelous relationship of all things.

Imagine this. . .

WE ARE ALL CONNECTED... Take a breath. Sooner or later you'll breathe a tiny particle that has been breathed by someone who came before you. By Michelangelo, George Washington, maybe Moses? (Jacob Bronowski, *The Ascent of Man*)

ONE BIG THOUGHT... Thanks to electron microscopes and modern physics we are now beginning to see that the universe more closely resembles one big thought rather than one big machine. Hmmm... (Sir James Jeans, British astronomer)

LOOKING AT GOD... Evidence has been found for the birth and evolution of the universe. The order is so amazing and the symmetry so beautiful that it seems there must be some design behind it. If you're religious, it's like looking at God...(George Smoot, Nobel Prize–winning physicist)

ALL ON A SPECK OF DUST... All the information we humans have taken time and energy to document over the ages can be written in the space of a cube one two-hundredth of an inch wide. Imagine it! That is the smallest bit of dust our eyes can even make out...(Richard Feynman, Nobel Prize–winning physicist)

BECAUSE life is what you make it…

BECAUSE no day ever repeats itself and no opportunity ever comes the same way again…

BECAUSE your talents long to show what they can do…

BECAUSE the right place and the right time are right where you are now…

BECAUSE you can be the difference…

BECAUSE there is beauty everywhere…

BECAUSE there is never a good reason to put off letting people know how much you love and appreciate them…

BECAUSE you never know how much time you have left…

BECAUSE at the end of life, you will be more disappointed by the things you didn't do than by the things you did do…

BECAUSE you are here and it is now…

There is no day more precious than the one you are living **now.**